The páramos of the higher altitudes of the Venezuelan Andes are typically represented by the "frailejón" (*Espeletia*) (ASTERACEAE) and the small tree "coloradito" (*Polylepis sericea*) (ROSACEAE). In this essentially herbaceous ecosystem we can find the tiny terrestrial orchid Pterichis multiflora.

At lower altitudes the cloud forest with its exuberant vegetation offers us a variety of beautiful plants such as the vine *Bomarea bredemeyerana* (ALSTROEMERIACEAE), *Anthurium* (ARACEAE) and many ferns and bamboos.

The páramos and *Espeletia*: pages 10 to 22.

Pterichis multiflora: page 23.

Polylepis sericea: page 24.

The cloud forest: pages 25 to 28.

Anthurium: page 27.

Bomarea bredemeyerana surrounded by ferns: page 28.

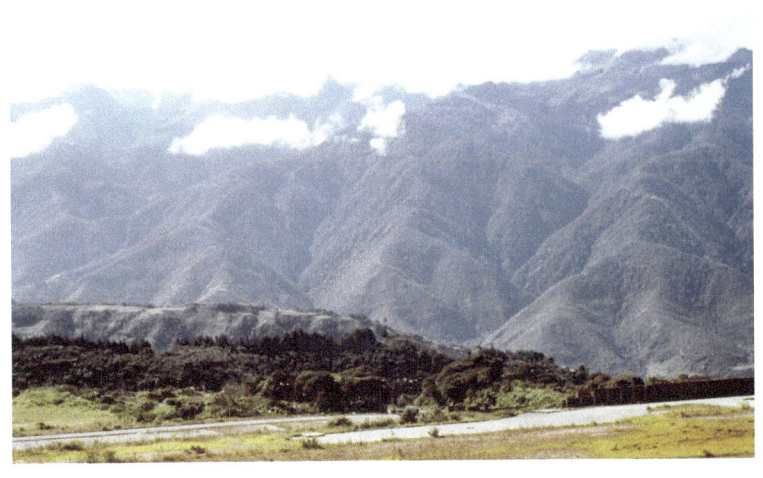

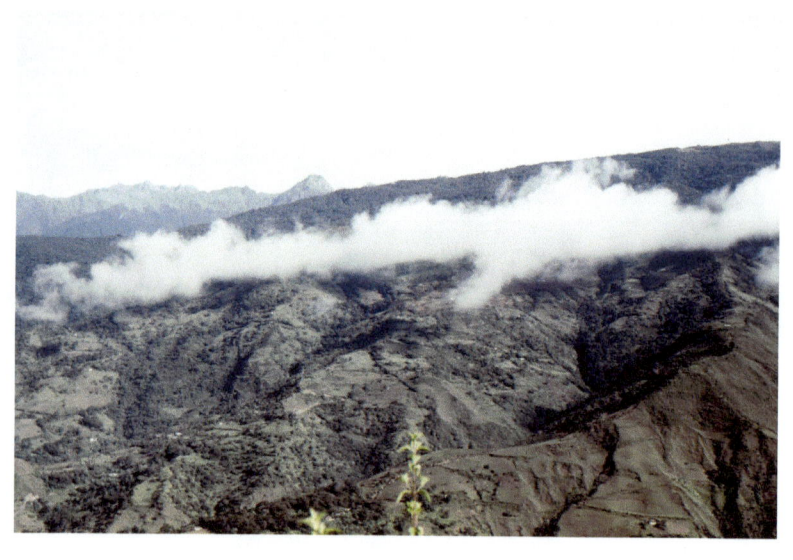

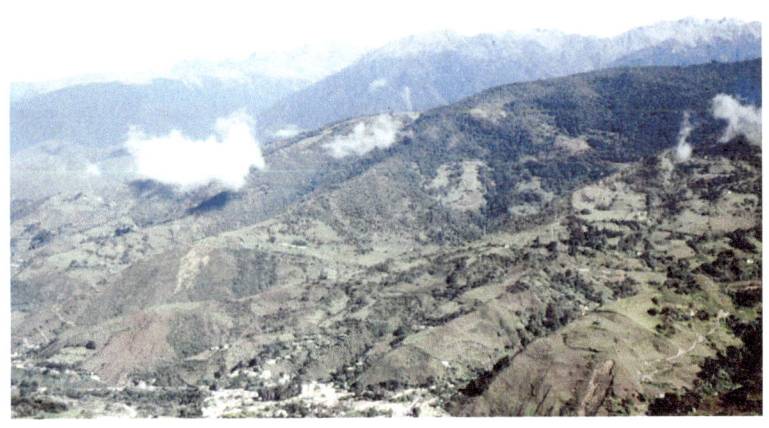

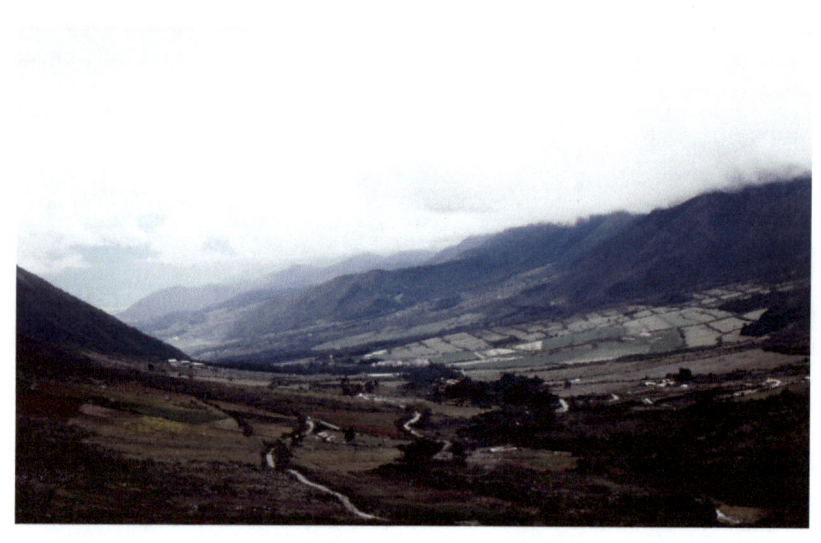

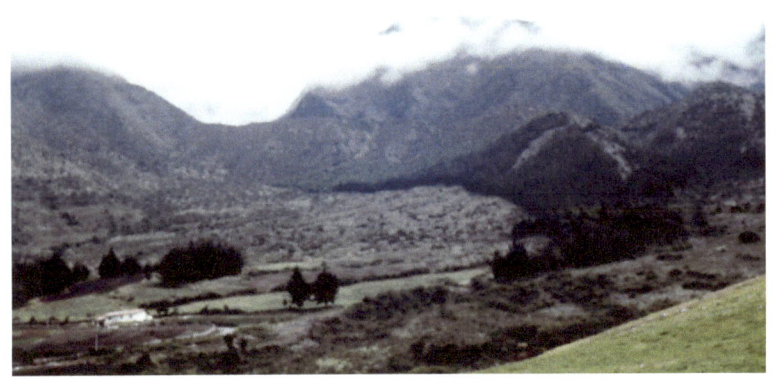

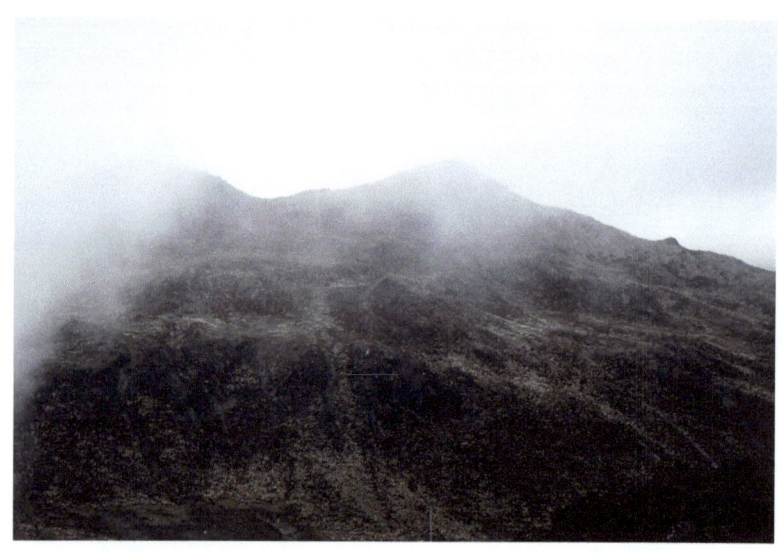

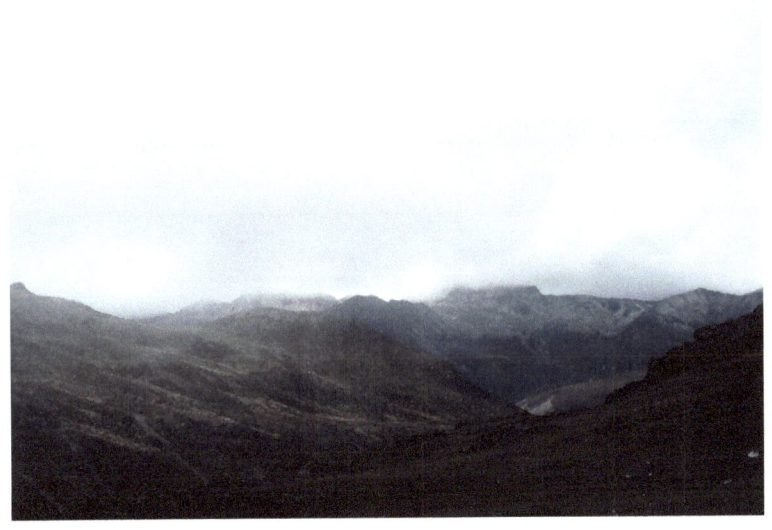

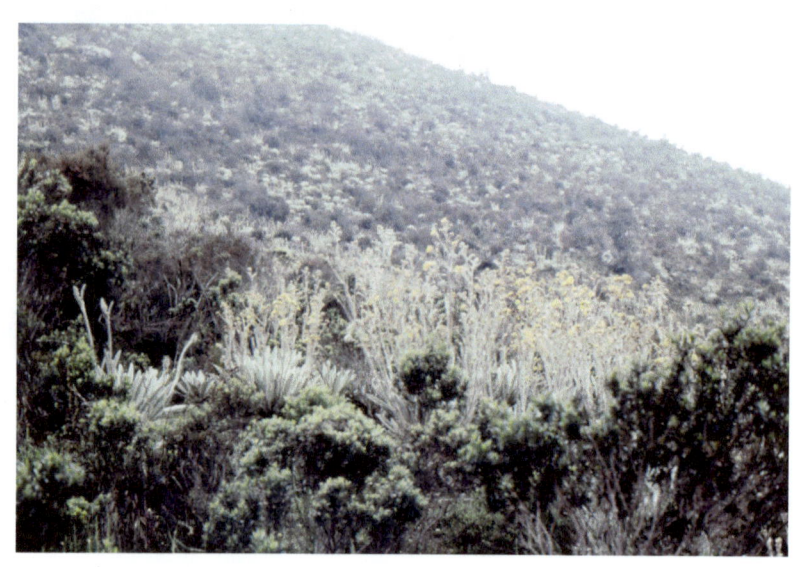

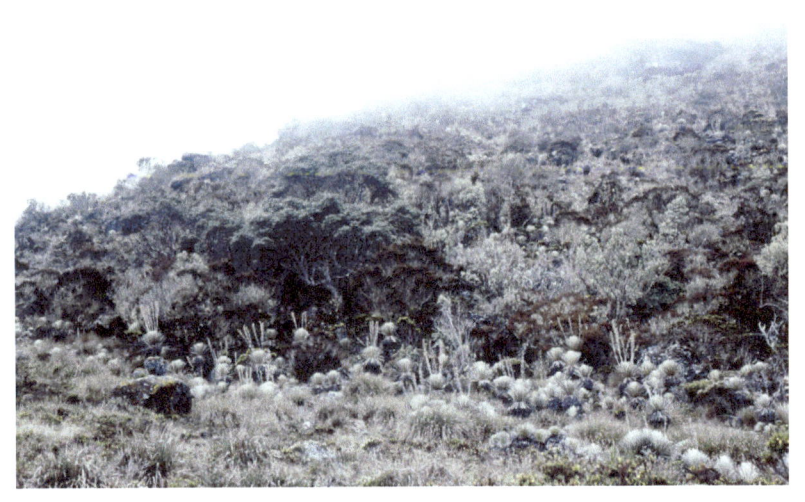

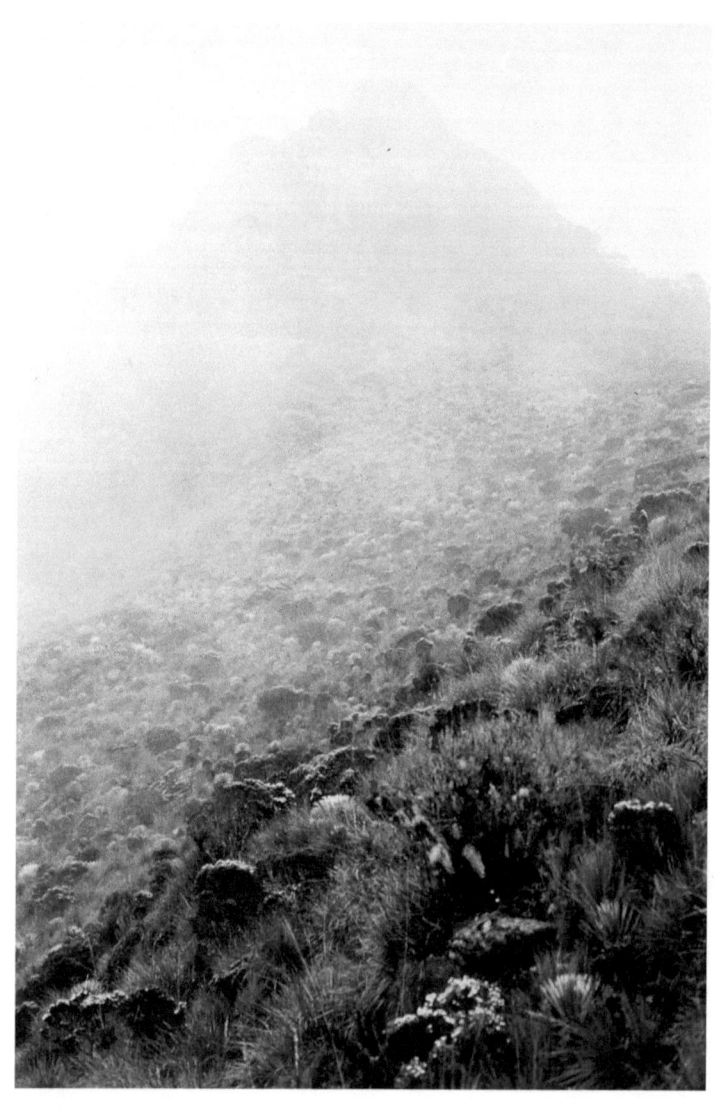

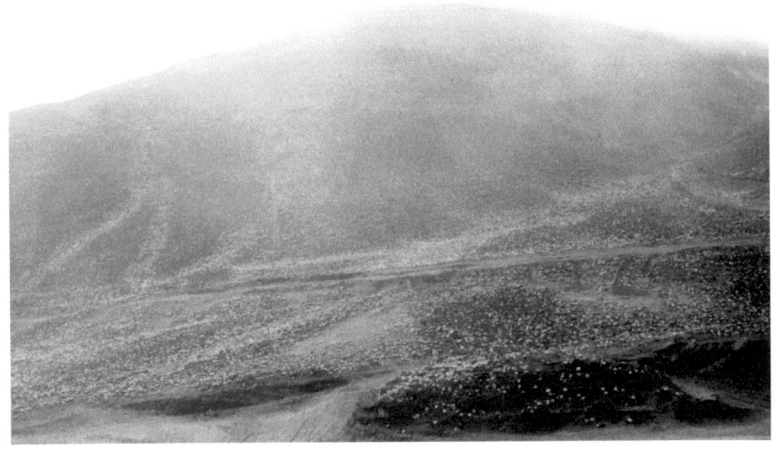

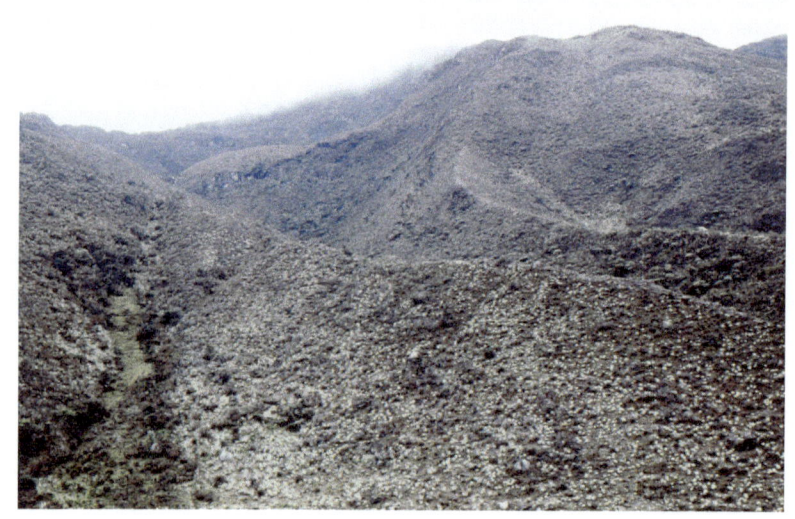

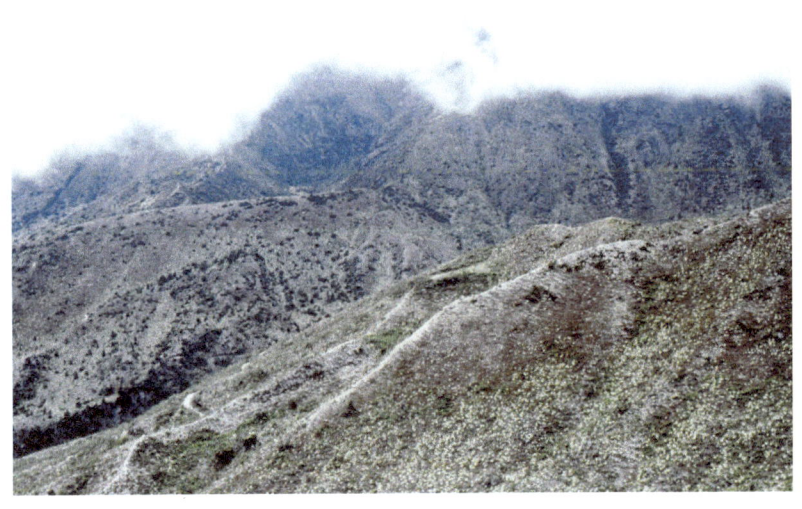

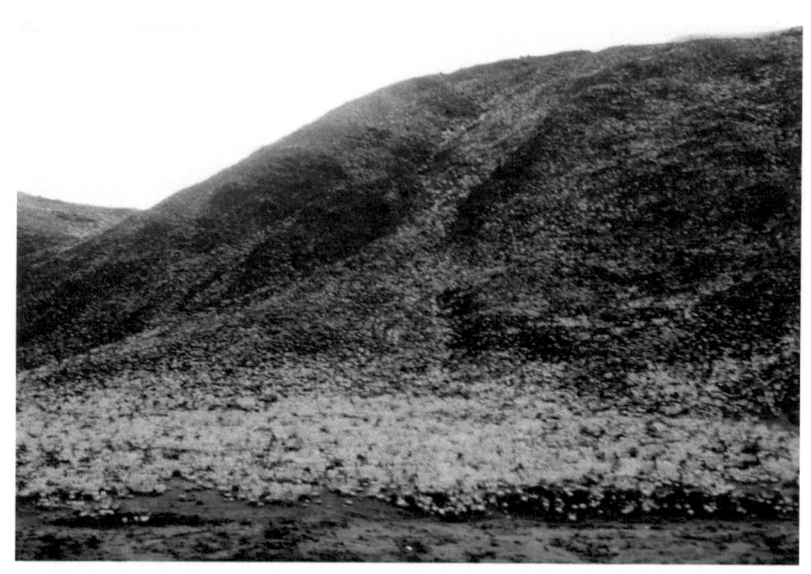

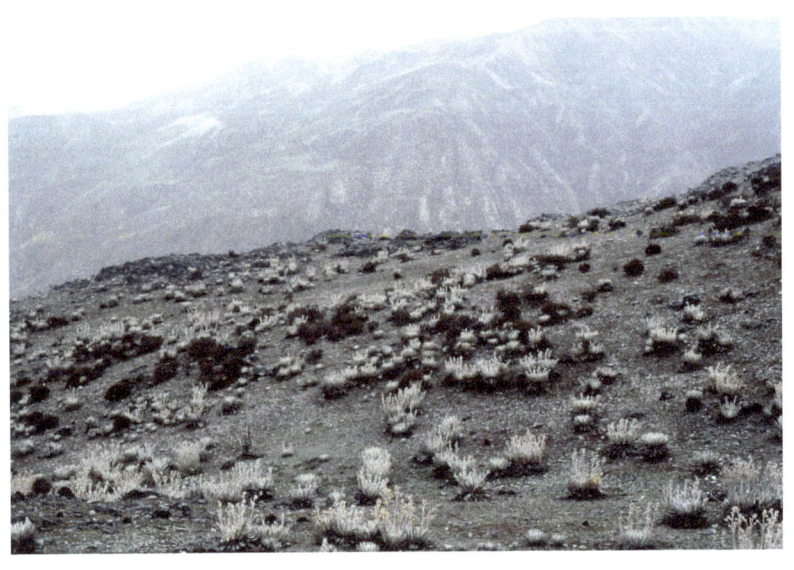

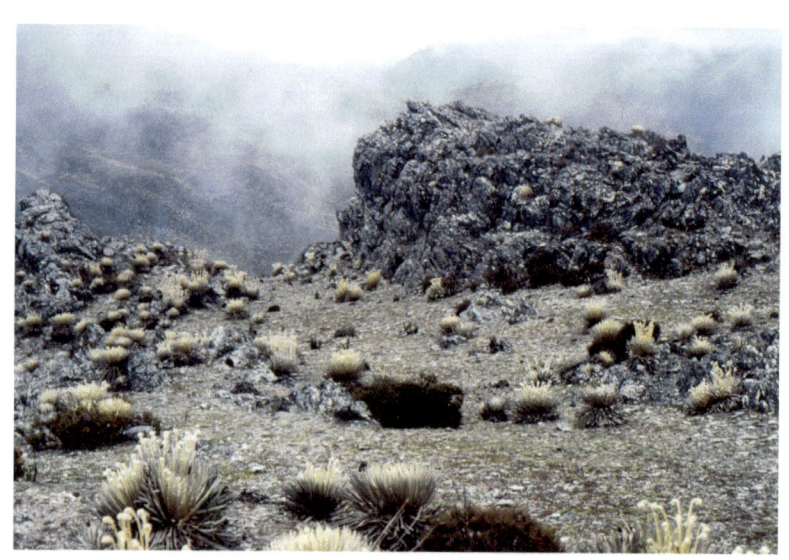

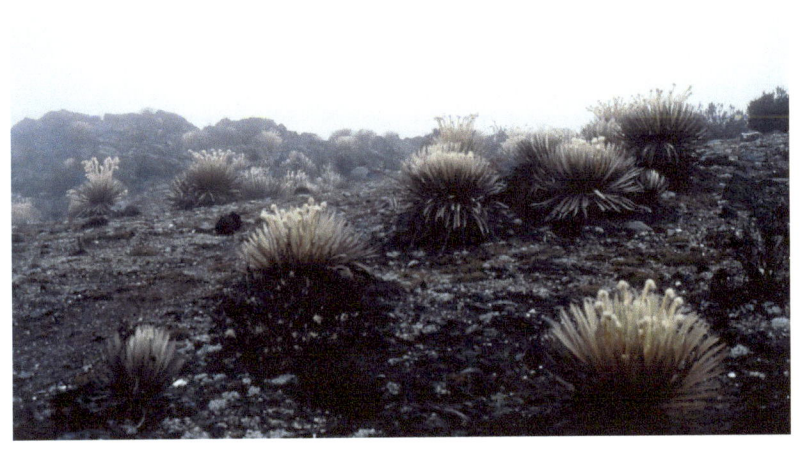

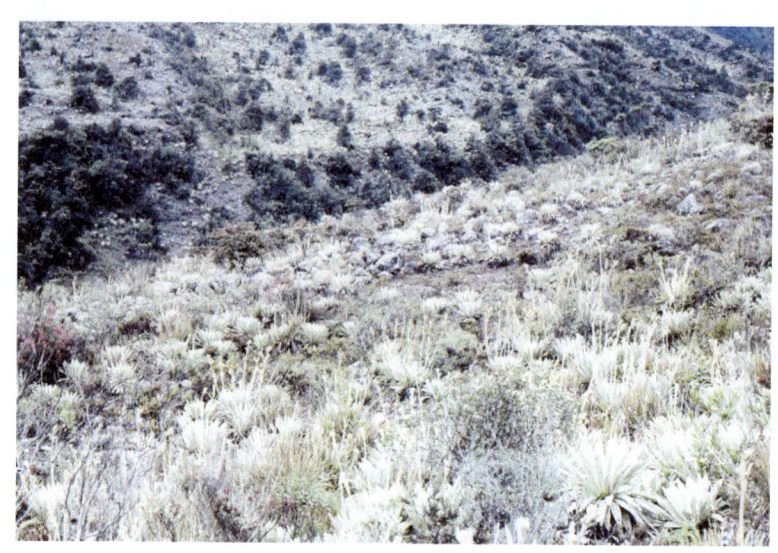

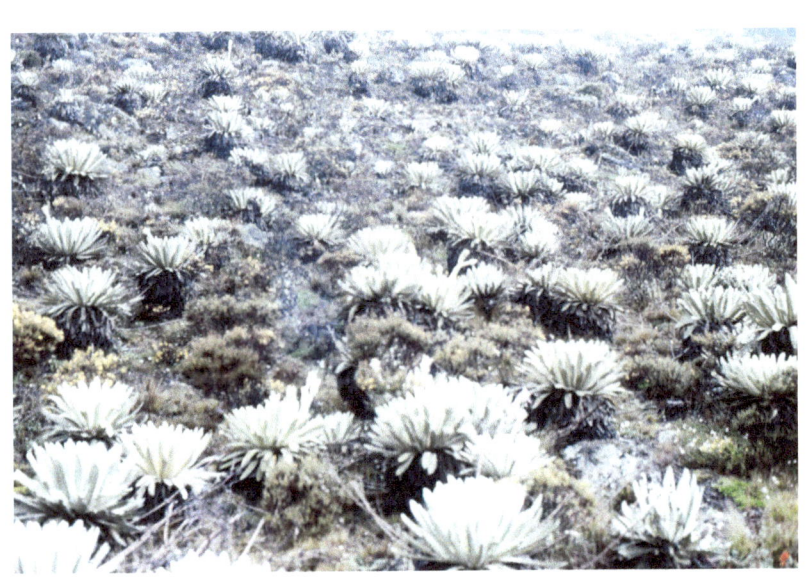

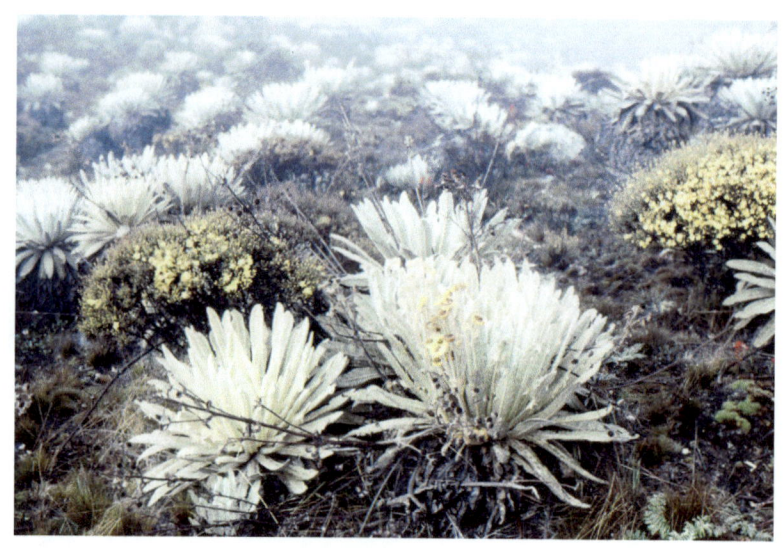

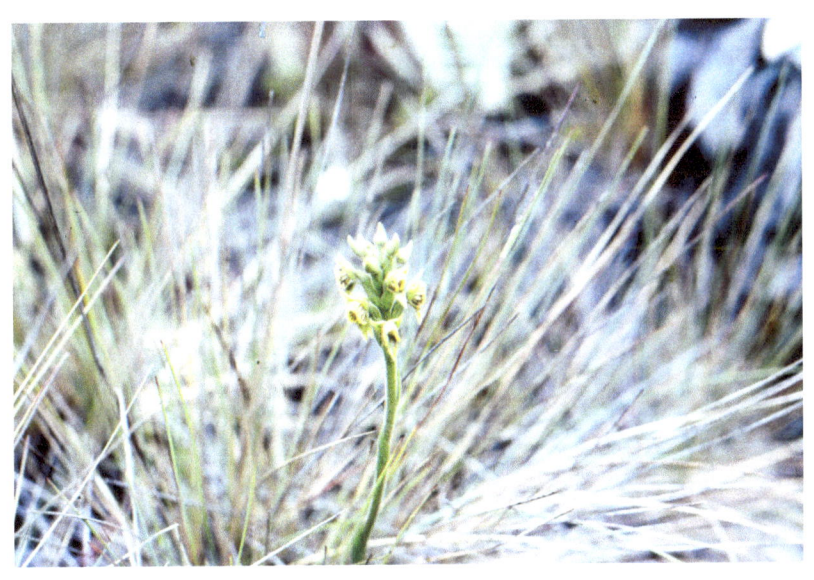

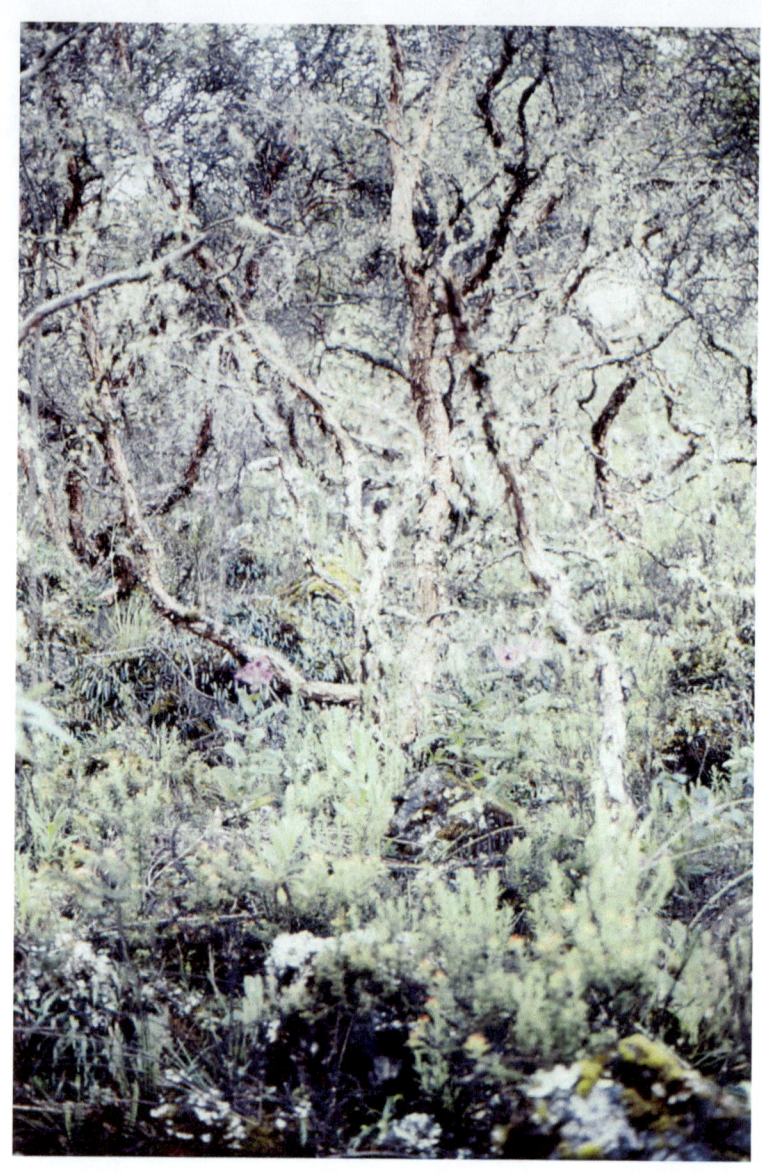

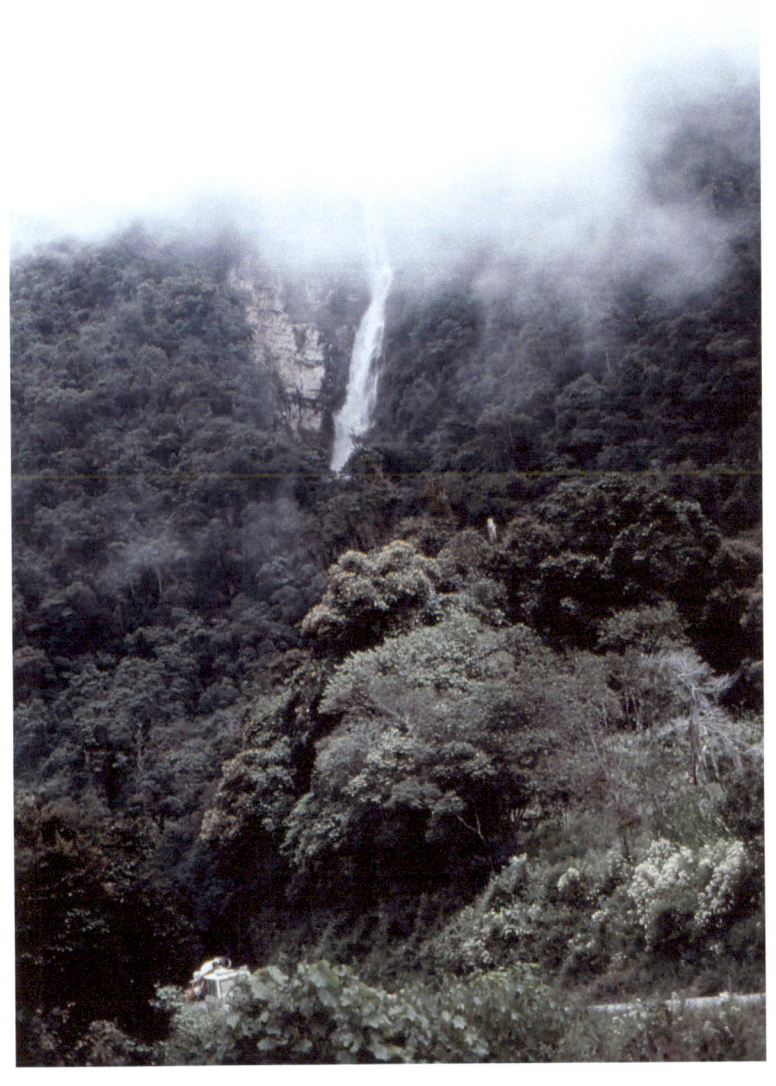

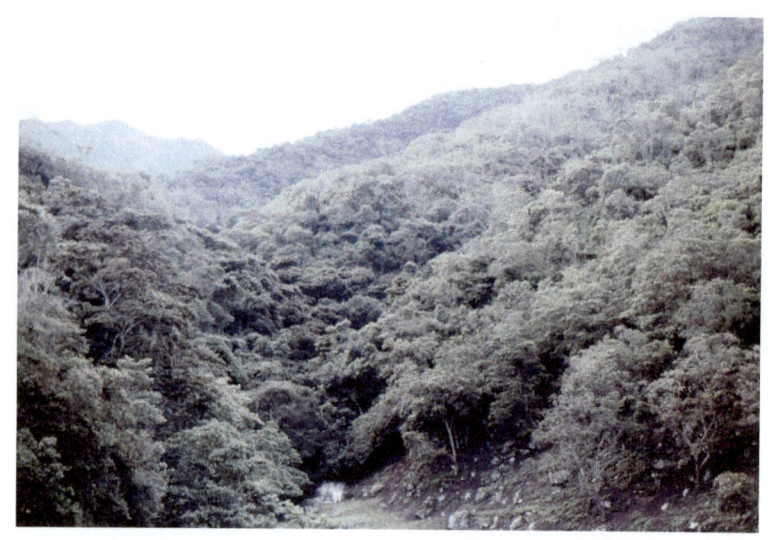

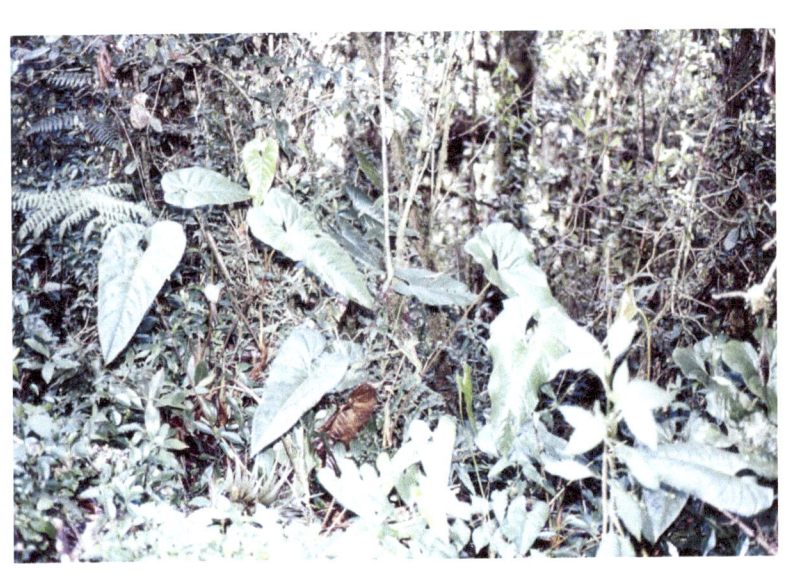

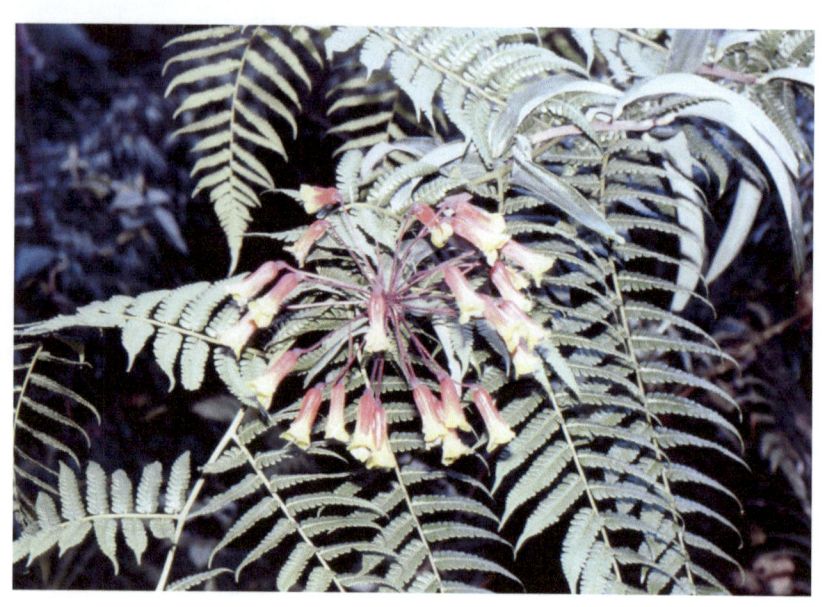

www.ingramcontent.com/pod-product-compliance
Lightning Source LLC
Chambersburg PA
CBHW040304220526
45473CB00002B/576